SHARKS

51 Fascinating, Crazy & Weird Facts

By TJ Rob

From the Fascinating, Crazy and Weird Animal Facts Series, Volume 2

ISBN 978-1-988695-33-4

Published by:
TJ Rob - www.TJRob.com
Suite 609
440-10816 Macleod Trail SE
Calgary, AB T2J 5N8

Photo Credits:
Images used under license from Shutterstock.com, Flickr.com, Pixabay.com, Creative Commons, Wikimedia Commons and Public Domain. Front Cover, Title Page – Photo by Terry Goss / Creative Commons, via Wikimedia Commons

Table of Contents

1. Do Sharks have a super sense of smell?

Great White Shark - Photo by Hermanus Backpackers via Wikimedia Commons

Sharks have been called "swimming noses" because their sense of smell is so good. A Shark's sense of smell is 10,000 times better than a Human's.

Sharks smell with their nostrils but don't breathe through them. They use their gills to breathe.

Great White Sharks can detect tiny amounts of blood from 3 miles away. If a Shark was put into a large Olympic swimming pool, it would be able to smell a single drop of blood in the water.

Some Sharks can tell which direction that smell is coming from.

2. How do Sharks hear when they have no ears?

Great White Shark – Photo by Sharkdiver.com, Public Domain

Hearing is probably the best of all of a Shark's senses. Some Sharks can hear prey in the water from 3,000 feet away. They are better at detecting low frequency sounds, so they can't detect the high-frequency sounds Dolphins make.

Never seen a Shark with ears?

Sharks have no visible ears. They only have an inner ear. Two holes on either side of a Shark's head might be the only clue that Sharks have ears.

Sound is often the Shark's first tip-off that prey is nearby. The prey doesn't even have to be that close.

Because sound travels farther and faster underwater, Sharks are easily able to detect their prey from far away. The sounds of splashing and the sounds of an injured prey create different sound frequencies that alert the Shark.

3. How well do Sharks see underwater?

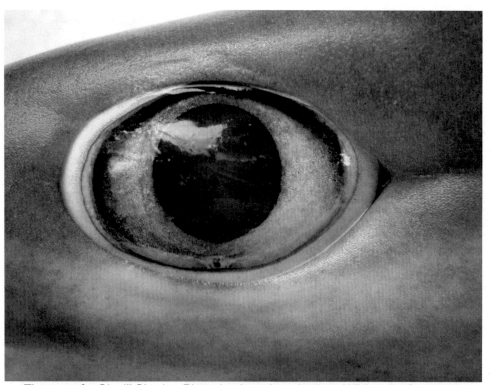

The eye of a Sixgill Shark – Photo by Jean-Lou Justine, Wikimedia Commons

Shark's eyes are on the sides of their heads. So they can see almost 360 degrees. They have only two blind spots: one in front of the snout and the other directly behind the head.

Do you know a Shark is the only fish that can blink with both eyes!

Sharks can see in murky water because of a special feature that makes their eyes more sensitive to light. A membrane in the back of the eye called the tapetum lucidum reflects sunlight back into the eye, so the Shark can make more use of what little light is there.

Sharks can also heat their eyes using a special system called retia next to a muscle in their eye socket, allowing them to continue hunting in ice cold waters.

Sharks that swim closer to the surface often have dark eyes to shield their eyes from the bright light.

Sharks are able to see colors. Divers have said for years that Sharks are attracted to certain colors, like the "yummy yellow" of some wetsuits. Scientists do know that some Sharks that live in well-lit environments have developed cone cells in their eyes that are just like the ones Humans use to distinguish different colors.

We don't know if Sharks prefer one color over another.

4. Do Sharks have any bones in their skeletons?

Dried Shark Fin showing cartilage - Photo by Natali Glado / Shutterstock.com

Sharks do not have a single bone in their bodies. Instead they have a skeleton made up of cartilage; the same type of tough, flexible tissue that makes up Human ears and noses.

Cartilage is an elastic tissue that is much softer than bones. When a Shark dies, salt from the ocean water completely dissolves its skeleton, leaving only the Shark's teeth behind.

5. What will happen if Sharks stop moving?

A Great White moving through the water – Photo by Elias Levy / Flickr.com

Some Sharks remain on the move for their entire lives. When they move, this forces water over their gills, delivering oxygen to the blood stream. If the Shark stops moving, then it will suffocate and die.

Great Whites, Mako Sharks and Salmon Sharks don't have the muscles they need to pump water through their mouth and over their gills. As long as they keep swimming, water keeps moving over their gills, keeping them alive.

6. If they have so many teeth, do Sharks get tooth cavities?

The lower jaw of a Great White showing the rows of teeth- Photo by Ryan Somma / Flickr.com

Shark teeth don't get cavities. This makes them strong and great for tearing prey.

Even though Sharks have rows and rows of razor-sharp teeth, they don't use their teeth to chew their prey. Shark teeth are strictly for snapping, gripping, crushing or ripping. The chunks of meat from the prey are swallowed whole.

Sharks have built-in toothpaste. The outer layer of Shark teeth is made of fluoride, which is used in toothpaste.

Sharks replace their teeth many times. Sharks don't lose teeth from cavities, but their teeth get stuck inside prey.

A Shark always has a row of smaller teeth developing behind its front teeth. Eventually the smaller teeth move forward, like a conveyor belt, and the front teeth fall out.

The average Shark has 40-45 teeth and can have up to seven rows of replacement teeth. Because Sharks lose a lot of teeth and grow them back quickly, they can have more than 30,000 teeth over their lifetime.

A Human adult has only 32 teeth.

7. Why do some Sharks have different shaped teeth?

All Sharks have slightly different teeth specifically designed for what they like to eat.

There are four types of teeth that Sharks can have.

Sharks like the Mako Shark eat mainly Fish. Makos have long, narrow, needle-like teeth ideal for gripping something as slippery and streamlined as a fish.

Sharp pointy teeth of the Sand Shark – Photo by Emmanuel Douzery/ Creative Commons via Wkimedia Commons.

Sharks like the Tiger Shark eat animals that have shells like crabs, Mussels, and Turtles. Tiger Sharks have thick, plate-like teeth perfect for crushing the shells of their prey.

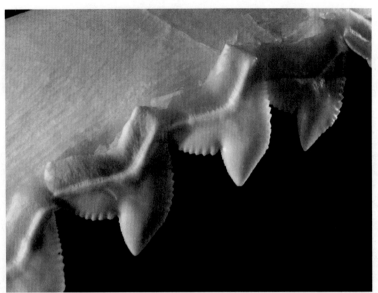

Thick Plate Teeth of the Tiger Shark – Photo by Stefan Kühn, CC BY-SA 3.0, Wikimedia Commons

Great White Sharks mainly eat Seals and other mammals. Great Whites have sharp, serrated cutting teeth for tearing off chunks of flesh.

Great White Tooth showing serrations- Photo by Kevmin, CC BY-SA 3.0, Wikimedia Commons

Finally, we have the gentle giants of the Shark family. Basking Sharks and Whale Sharks eat Krill and other forms of Plankton. While they have many teeth, they are tiny and useless, as these Sharks feed by filtering water through their gills.

Whale Shark feeding- Photo by KAZ2.0 / Flickr.com

8. How many species of Shark are there today?

The Most Common Sharks found today - Image by tonynetone / Flickr.com

When you hear the word "Shark", you likely imagine a picture of a Great White or a Hammerhead Shark. There are actually 500 Shark species (perhaps even more) roaming the world's oceans today.

They vary in size and even shape, from only 7 inches to over 40 feet long. Some are weird looking like a Hammerhead to the best known Great White Shark.

They all share similar body characteristics like large livers, skeletons made of cartilage and super senses like hearing, smell and sight.

Over the last thirty years, almost 250 species of Sharks have been discovered. Who knows how many species haven't been found!

9. Do you know these Great White Sharks facts?

A Great White Shark feeding - Photo by Fallows C, Gallagher AJ, via Wikimedia Commons

- Great whites are the deadliest Shark in the ocean. These powerful predators can race through the water at 20 miles per hour.
- Surfers are often attacked by Great Whites. From beneath the surface, a Great White might mistake the surf board's outline for that of a Seal, Walrus or Sea Lion.
- Great white Sharks off the coast of Seal Island, South Africa, are known to jump almost 10 feet in the air to catch unsuspecting Seals. They hit Seals with as much force as a car crash, stunning them before chowing down.
- Great Whites are known to be man-eaters, even though they do not like the taste of Humans. They often bite and release attack victims.
- These Sharks are really picky eaters. Their diet requires lots of fat, and after one bite a Great White Shark can decide whether or not the meal will satisfy its nutritional needs. If it doesn't, the Shark will leave the rest and swim away.

- A Great White Shark can fast as long as three months after a big meal.
- The Shark's body helps its speed and helps it easily glide through the water, so it was thought that this would be helpful in the design of submarines.
- Unlike other species of Shark, the Great White is warm-blooded, so it is able to regulate its own body temperature. Other Sharks rely on the temperature of the water to regulate their own temperatures. In order to regulate its temperature, the Great White needs to eat a lot of meat.

10. What was the biggest Shark that ever lived?

Prehistoric underwater scene showing a Megalodon Shark eating a Blue Whale – Image by Elenarts / Shutterstock.com

The prehistoric Shark Megalodon probably grew to over 60 feet long. Megalodons lived from about 20 million years ago but went extinct about 1.6 million years ago. At 3 times the size of the biggest Great Whites, they were the largest and most powerful Shark that ever lived.

Megalodon chomped on Whales, with the most powerful bite of any animal that's ever lived. A Great White Shark bite has 1.8 tons of force, but the Megalodon used up to 18.2 tons of bite force – more than 10 times more!

11. What is special about the Shark Immune System?

Researchers tagging a young Thresher Shark - photo by NOAA, Public Domain, Wikimedia Commons

Do you know whose immune system is strongest among all animals? Sharks! They are the healthiest as they are immune to almost all known diseases.

The average Shark lives to be 25 years old, but some can get as old as 100! They live so long because their chances of contracting a disease are low.

Their skeleton is made up entirely of cartilage, which drastically lowers the likelihood of developing a tumor and strengthens their immunity.

Barnacles and bacteria do not usually grow on Sharks. Scientists want to use Shark skin to treat bacterial infections in people.

Shark corneas are being used in Human eye transplants.

Sharks are immune to some forms of cancer, so scientists want to study Sharks to understand how to maybe find a cure for the disease.

12. How often do Sharks attack humans?

Great White Shark showing its teeth - Photo by wp Kommunikáció / Flickr.com

As sensational as Shark attack newspaper headlines are, the reality is that you are more likely to be bitten by another person than a Shark.

Most Shark attacks on humans occur within a few hundred yards of shore, because that is where people are most likely to be.

More than eighty percent of people who are bitten by Sharks live to tell the tale.

Thousands of people enter the ocean on a daily basis for swimming, diving, snorkeling and boating among many other activities. Maybe even in places where there are Sharks all the time! Yet there is only an average of 30 to 50 Shark attacks reported each year. Only 5 to 12 are fatal. This proves that Sharks do not eat people. If they did, there would be hundreds of people dying every month – which does not happen.

More people are killed every year by falling coconuts in Asia alone, than people being killed by Sharks around the world. You are more likely to be killed by a falling coconut than killed by a Shark. Roughly 150 people are killed each year by coconuts compared to Sharks killing only 5 to 12 people a year. Coconuts are more dangerous than Sharks!

While many people fear Sharks and think of them as one of the world's most aggressive and deadly animals, the chances of dying from a Shark attack fall well below the chances of being killed by hornets, wasps, bees or dogs.

13. Do you know these Shark facts?

Blacktip Shark - Photo by David Stanley/ Flickr.com

- As long as a Shark's back is mostly under water, it can swim easily. A nine-foot-long bull Shark can swim in just two feet of water.
- Portuguese Sharks live at depths of 12,000 feet, which is over two miles deep.
- Before sandpaper was invented, people used the rough skin of Sharks to smooth and polish wood.
- Japanese warriors wrapped Shark skin around the handles of their swords to keep the swords from slipping out of their hands.
- Sharks can be found in all of Earth's oceans.

14. Are Whale Sharks dangerous to Humans?

Whale Shark diving - Photo by Marcel Ekkel / Flickr.com

Whale Sharks are 3 times larger than the average Shark, but don't be afraid of these gentle creatures. Although most species of Shark are less than 3 feet long, the Whale Shark can grow to 50 feet long. Whale Sharks are the world's largest fish that live in our oceans today.

They are filter feeders that use their many rows of teeth to gather Plankton. Whale Sharks are no threat to Humans. Divers love being in the water with them.

The Whale Shark's mouth stretches up to 15 feet wide, the largest mouth of all Shark species.

15. What is special about Greenland Sharks?

The rare Greenland Shark - Photo by Justin / Flickr.com

Greenland Sharks are rarely seen by Humans because they live in very deep water – at depths of 2,000 feet and more. No one had photographed this Shark in its natural environment until 1995.

They are the northern most Shark, and live in the oceans around Greenland, Northern Canada and Iceland. Greenland Sharks prefer near freezing waters.

They are similar in size to Great White Sharks.

Greenland Sharks can swim-dive to over 7,200 feet below the surface. They are also the slowest moving of all Sharks, with a top speed of only 1.6 miles per hour.

Unlike most Shark meat, Greenland Shark flesh is highly poisonous and must be boiled three times before eating. Preparation of Greenland Shark meat takes five months and is a delicacy in Greenland.

Many Greenland Sharks have small parasites on their eyes that glow in dark water. Scientists think these glowing parasites attract prey into the Sharks' mouths. These parasites eat the cornea in the Shark's eyes, making them partially blind. Luckily for the

Shark, light does not get down to the deep waters where the Greenland Shark lives. So it relies on other senses to get around and find prey.

16. How long have Sharks been on Earth?

An Oceanic White Tip Shark with Pilot Fish - Photo by OldakQuill, Wikimedia Commons

What's older than Sharks? Almost nothing. Sharks have been swimming in the ocean for more than 400 million years. They predate practically everything that has a spine, including Humans and Dinosaurs.

Shark body design has remained basically the same for the last 140 million years.

Sharks have survived 5 massive planet extinction events. These extinction events killed most life on earth. The last one around 65 million years ago killed the Dinosaurs. But not Sharks.

They are here to stay.

17. What determines the size of Sharks?

Live Dwarf Lantern Shark - Photo by Javontaevious, CC BY-SA 3.0, Wikimedia Commons

The size of a Shark species relates to where they hunt: Smaller Sharks tend to feed near the ocean floor, and larger Sharks hunt in the middle depths and near the surface, where they can more easily snatch larger prey such as Seals.

If the Whale Shark is the largest species at 50 feet long, then Dwarf Lantern Sharks are among the tiniest!

They measure an average of 8 to 10 inches in length and can make their own light, a phenomenon that's especially helpful as Dwarf Lantern Sharks will dive more than 1,000 feet underwater to hunt.

18. Why are Hammerhead Sharks so weird looking?

The Great Hammerhead Shark – Photo by Jurgen Leckie / Flickr.com

Hammerhead Sharks are famous for their oddly shaped heads, called cephalofoils. The electrical sensors the Sharks use to pinpoint their prey are spread out along the cephalofoil's wide surface area, giving them better prey detection skills. This makes them better hunters.

There are actually 10 different species of Hammerhead Sharks, with the Great Hammerhead being the largest and most common.

Hammerhead Sharks' heads are soft at birth so they won't jam the mothers' birth canals.

Hammerheads have small mouths relative to their body size and do a lot of bottom-hunting. They are also known to form schools during the day, sometimes in groups of over 100. At night Hammerhead Sharks tend to leave their schools and hunt alone.

Sharks tan too. Some Hammerheads swim near the ocean's surface since darker skin means better camouflage.

Great Hammerhead Sharks are nomadic and have been known to roam all the way from the coasts of Florida to the Polar Regions. This lets them take advantage of rising and falling water temperatures in different parts of the ocean.

19. Why should Sharks fear us more than we fear them?

A Silky Shark caught on a sport fishing line - Photo by Álvaro Quintero, CC BY-SA 2.0, Wikimedia Commons

While many of us have learned to fear Sharks, they're the ones who should fear us. People are Sharks' deadliest predator. In fact, Humans kill more than 100 million Sharks each year.

Sharks may seem like a permanent part of the ocean, but according to the World Conservation Union, 20% to 30% of Sharks are close to extinction.

The main reason for the drop in Shark numbers is Shark finning. Shark fin soup is a delicacy in China and is served at important events, like weddings and anniversaries. So Sharks need to be caught in huge numbers.

Shark finning refers to fishing Sharks for their fins. Fishermen catch the Sharks and cut off their fins and throw the rest of the Shark's body back into ocean. Sharks that are thrown back into the ocean without their fins are often still alive are not able to move without their fins. They sink to the bottom of the ocean and die of suffocation or are eaten by other predators.

Because of overfishing and Shark finning, some populations of certain Shark species have been reduced down by approximately 90%.

Overfishing can have a dangerous effect on Sharks.

For example: The Whale Shark can only start reproducing from the age of 30! Unfortunately, because of overfishing many Sharks don't reach maturity to help replace the Sharks that have been already caught.

A Great White Shark being fed bait - Photo by Elias Levy / Flickr.com

20. How do Sharks sense that you are in the water?

Diving with Sharks - Photo by Manoel Lemos / Flickr.com

Sharks can hear the sound of their prey from more than 3000 feet away. Sound waves travel fast and far in water, so Sharks have no trouble picking up low-pitched noises from movements such as fish schools, swimmers and even Coast Guard helicopters flying low over the ocean.

Sharks can also use heartbeats to track their prey. Sharks have nodules on their noses about the size of a pimple, called ampullae of Lorenzini. These nodules sense electricity, so the electrical pulses that come from a beating heart can act like a beacon for nearby Sharks. Active Sharks have up to 1,500 Ampullae of Lorenzi.

Sharks are able to notice the smallest changes in the electricity conducted through saltwater. All living things give off the tiniest charge of electricity. Blood in the water changes its conductivity of electricity in the water. So, Sharks don't see blood and attack: They can sense and smell it.

21. Is the stomach the largest organ in a Shark's body?

A Lemon Shark – Photo by Albert Kok, CC BY-SA 3.0, Wikimedia Commons

The liver, not the stomach is the largest organ in a Shark's body. The liver can be 25% of the Shark's weight.

Unlike fish, Sharks do not have a swim bladder to keep them afloat— instead Sharks have a large filled liver.

Sharks' livers contain lots of oil.

Sharks that spend a lot of time on the surface have a massive liver - like Whale Sharks and Basking Sharks.

Shark liver oil used to be the main source of Vitamin A for Humans.

The liver of a basking Shark can weigh over 1,800 pounds and contain 600 gallons of oil.

22. Do Sharks eat in the middle of the day?

Shark eating a fish – Photo by annca / Public Domain

Sharks don't follow the same three meals-a-day eating schedule as Humans, they eat when they find food, no matter what time it is.

A common myth is that Sharks don't attack in the middle of the day.

And that may be true — but it's likely because most beachgoers get out of the water to rest or eat at lunchtime, so there aren't as many people around to cross paths with Sharks at that time of the day.

23. What Shark is called the "garbage can" of the sea?

A Tiger Shark - Photo by Albert Kok, CC BY-SA 3.0, Wikimedia Commons

The Tiger Shark is nicknamed the "garbage can of the sea" because it will eat anything. Garbage like old license plates, gasoline tanks and tires have been found in its stomach. The Tiger Shark is the second-most dangerous Shark in the world.

For Tiger Shark moms-to-be, two different uteri are the key to giving birth to at least two pups.

Before they're even born, Tiger Shark pups eat their twin brothers and sisters!

This may seem cruel, but they are just seeking out nutrients to sustain themselves as they grow. The first Tiger Shark pup to hatch inside its mother's womb devours its unborn siblings until only two pups remain, one on each side of the womb.

24. Do all Sharks live in the ocean?

Bull Shark - Photo by William Eburn, CC BY 2.5, Wikimedia Commons

Did you think you had to be swimming in the ocean to meet a Shark? Think again.

Bull Sharks like both freshwater and salt water. They have been seen in bays, lagoons and even rivers, sometimes thousands of miles inland.

How do these Sharks survive in freshwater?

Their bodies have evolved to handle both salty and fresh water.

They take in extra water and urinate into the freshwater around them, at a rate over 20 times faster than the average saltwater Shark! This does mean their kidneys have to work extra hard to filter the freshwater, and they use up a lot of energy - so Bull Sharks have great appetites.

25. How rare is the Megamouth Shark?

Megamouth Shark - Photo by FLMNH, CC BY-SA 4.0, Wikimedia Commons

One of the rarest Sharks is the Megamouth Shark.

Fewer than 100 specimens of the beast have ever been seen. It was first discovered in 1976 when one was struck by and got tangled in the anchor of a Navy ship off Hawaii. This Shark can grow up to 15 feet long and is a filter feeder, sucking in Plankton from the ocean.

The Megamouth Shark wasn't discovered by scientists until 1976, and there have only been 41 known sightings of the species. Like Whale Sharks, the Megamouth Sharks have huge jaws that extend past their eyes. The mouth can reach up to 3 feet across, while the rest of the body is about 16 feet long.

26. Why are Sharks important?

Bull Sharks - Photo by amanderson2 / Flickr.com

Sharks play a very important role in marine communities and help maintain the delicate balance of life.

Many Shark species keep other marine animal populations in check.

Some Sharks feed on the sick and weak, which helps prey populations to stay healthy.

Like Lions on land, Sharks are at the top of the food chain in the underwater jungle. Sharks eating habits affect the populations of all sea life below them.

For example: Without Great Hammerhead Sharks, Octopus populations would jump, which would then decrease the number of Lobsters, since they are one of the Octopus' favorite snacks. This is just one of 500 Shark species.

27. I bet you didn't know these Shark facts...

Great White breaching the water - Photo by Lwp Kommunikáció / Flickr.com

- Sharks are silent killers. They don't make vocal sounds because they don't have vocal cords.
- Native Americans in Florida used the teeth of Great White Sharks as arrowheads.
- Sharks do not have scales. Instead their skin is covered with denticles, which give the skin its roughness. As Sharks grow, the denticles fall off and are replaced by larger ones.
- A pair of shoes made of Shark leather can last four times longer than shoes made with regular leather.

28. Are all Sharks Man-Eaters?

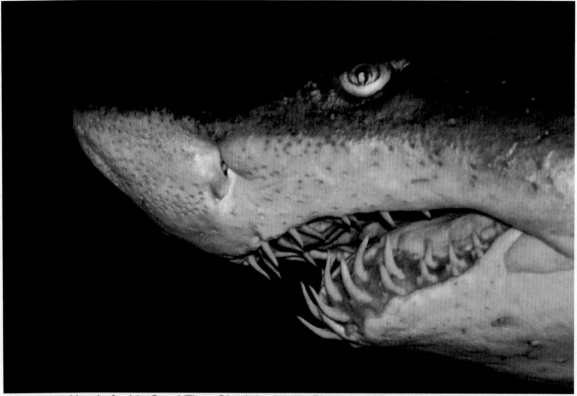

Head of a big Sand Tiger Shark in detail - Photo by MP cz / Shutterstock.com

Humans are not food for Sharks.

You may think of Sharks as hungry, man-eating terrors of the sea, but in reality, only 3% of the more than 500 species of Shark — a small minority — are known to attack Humans.

When an attack does occur, it's most likely that the Shark has mistaken the Human for its actual prey (a Seal, for example). Most of the time, a curious Shark takes a bite to determine if this is food. The Sharks involved in incidents with Humans are often hunting for similar-sized prey to Humans, such as Seals or Dolphins.

The majority of Shark species actually eat fish or invertebrates, such as Squid or Clams. There's a diversity of feeding behaviors: large filter feeders, such as the Whale Shark, strain Plankton through modified gills, while bottom-dwelling suction feeders, such as the Nurse Shark, appear to "inhale" food into their mouths.

29. How fast can the fastest Shark swim?

The fastest Shark - The Shortfin Mako Shark - Photo by jidanchaomian / Flickr.com

The Shortfin Mako Shark is the fastest species of Shark known to date and can swim up to 65mph!

That's way faster than any Human could ever swim. It's as fast as the speed limit on some freeways! The Shortfin Mako Shark can accelerate faster than a Porsche.

Shortfin Makos are also able to leap 20 feet above the surface of the water. To do that they have to reach a speed of 20 miles per hour or even faster!

All Sharks have cruising speeds, but when chasing fish or fleeing from an enemy they can swim much faster.

Sharks can't stop quickly, and they cannot swim backwards.

30. Are Sharks Cold Blooded or Warm Blooded creatures?

Great White Shark - Photo by Travelbag Ltd / Flickr.com

Almost all Sharks are "ectothermic", which is a fancy way of calling them cold-blooded.

They are unable to regulate their own body temperature. Instead, it is determined by the surrounding environment. That is why most Sharks like to stay in temperate or tropical waters, rather than Polar environments - although there are some cold-water Sharks like the Greenland Shark.

There are some Sharks, like the Mako, the Great White, the Salmon Shark, the Basking Shark and the Big Eye Thresher Shark, that are partially warm-blooded.

These Sharks can raise their temperature above the temperature of the water when they need to have occasional short bursts of speed in hunting. Warm blooded Sharks are able to contract their muscles faster for greater strength and speed. They are also able to extend their range into much colder water too.

31. Are all Sharks grey in color?

Leopard Shark - Photo by Cliff / Flickr.com

Not all Sharks are grey in color. Many Sharks are quite colorful.

Sharks that live on the seafloor are often camouflaged with spots, stripes, bars or blotches so that they are hidden among plants and stones on the sand.

Many Sharks that hunt near the sea's surface are counter-shaded. This means they have dark backs which makes them difficult to see if you are looking down at them. They also have white bellies which makes them hard to see if you are underwater and looking up at them.

Sharks that live in the deep ocean may be almost black but some, like the Greenland Shark and the Megamouth Shark, have body parts that glow in the dark to attract their prey to them.

32. Can Sharks eat all Fish?

The Moses Sole Fish - Photo by prilfish / Flickr.com

There are some things a Shark cannot eat, such as a small flat fish called the Moses Sole.

When a Shark bites a Moses Sole, it releases a chemical in the Shark's mouth that makes the Shark release it.

Scientists are trying to duplicate this chemical so it can be used to keep Sharks away from people.

33. Have you ever seen a flat-as-a-pancake Shark?

The Angel Shark - Photo by RYO SATO / Flickr.com

Some Sharks, like the Angel Shark, are so flat that they look like they're part of the sea floor.

The flat bodies of these unusual Sharks look more like a Stingray than a Shark. They can range in colors anywhere from a light brown to a light grey with white markings.

This variety of coloring is what allows the Angel Shark to camouflage itself as it will match the colors of the sand it swims near.

When they hunt, they bury themselves into the sandy or muddy bottom and wait for prey to come by.

34. Is this one of the ugliest Sharks?

The Goblin Shark - Photo by Dianne Bray, CC BY 3.0 au, via Wikimedia Commons

Some scientists call it "FrankenShark" because it looks so ugly.

The Goblin Shark has a long snout, beady eyes and pink-gray flabby skin.

Goblin Sharks were first discovered in Japan in 1898.

Its weird snout may be a step in evolution toward something like a Saw Shark or Hammerhead Shark.

Making the Goblin Shark look even stranger is it's slim, flabby body and pink coloring.

The pink coloring is due to the blood vessels beneath the skin that show through.

The pink color becomes darker as the Shark grows older, so young Sharks may actually look white.

35. What is the laziest of all Sharks?

Nurse Sharks – Photo by Skeeze / Public Domain

Nurse Sharks are probably the laziest Sharks. They spend most of the day resting on the sandy sea floor, sometimes stacked on top of each other.

Nurse Sharks are able to breathe while stationary by pumping water through their mouths and out their gills.

Nurse Sharks only use about 18% of the energy that very active Sharks such as the Shortfin Mako Shark use.

When they get hungry, Nurse Sharks are like giant vacuum cleaners, sucking prey off the sea floor or from between rocks.

36. What Shark has the longest tail in proportion to its body length?

Thresher Shark - Photo by Petter Lindgren, CC BY-SA 3.0, Wikimedia Commons

The Thresher Shark uses its long tail to fish. The long tail, which can be as long as the body of the Shark itself, is where the Thresher Shark gets its name. These Sharks can grow up to 20 feet long, so their tails can be almost as long too.

A Thresher Shark will use its tail to swat at smaller fish to stun them before feeding. These Sharks will also "slap" the water in order to herd the prey into larger groups to make it easier to capture its dinner.

These are very athletic Sharks. Thresher Sharks are one of the few species of Shark that are known to jump fully out of the water, which is called breaching.

37. What is the Shark with the weirdest name?

The Banded Wobbegong Shark - Photo by Sylke Rohrlach / Flickr.com

The Wobbegong Shark has a very weird name for a Shark. It gets its name from an Australian aboriginal language. Wobbegong means shaggy beard which refers to the growths around the mouths of the Shark. Wobbegong Sharks are well camouflaged with a symmetrical pattern of bold markings which resemble a carpet.

Wobbegong is the common name given to the 12 species of Carpet Sharks. They are found in the shallow temperate and tropical waters of the Western Pacific Ocean and Eastern Indian Ocean.

Wobbegongs are bottom-dwelling Sharks, so spend much of their time resting on the sea floor. The Wobbegongs are ambush predators, lying hidden on the seabed until prey approaches.

Most species have a maximum length of 4 feet or less, but the largest, the Spotted Wobbegong, and the Banded Wobbegong, can reach about 9 feet in length.

38. And what about these Shark facts?

Feeding Caribbean Sharks - Photo by Joi Ito / Flickr.com

- Sharks want variety in their diets too. In an aquarium, a Shark will refuse food if it has eaten the same thing too many times.
- Sharks have some of the largest brains among fish
- In aquariums, Sharks bond with staff. Sharks behave differently with Humans they know well than they do with strangers.
- When a Shark eats food that it can't digest (like a turtle shell or tin can), it can vomit by thrusting its stomach out its mouth then pulling it back in.

39. How are baby Sharks born?

Baby Blacktip Reef Sharks swimming in shallow water – Photo by bettyx1138 / Flickr.com

Exactly how a Shark comes into the world depends on its species.

Baby Sharks are called pups.

Not all species of Shark give birth to live pups. Some species lay an egg case on the ocean floor and the pup hatches later on its own. Some Sharks start working before they're even born, chewing their way out of their egg to enter the open ocean. These tough, leathery pouches protect the eggs while the Sharks are growing. These egg cases are sometimes called "mermaid's purses."

Most Sharks are born alive (viviparous). There are two ways a pup can grow inside the mother. In some Sharks, the embryos feed on the yolk attached to their bellies.

Other species have an umbilical cord that connects to a mother's blood supply. A mother Shark can give birth to up to 48 pups in one litter.

The pups are usually born tail first and might rest beside their mother for a while before swimming away to fend for themselves. A pup is born ready to take care of itself.

40. How long are mother Sharks pregnant?

Baby Shark - Photo by Hillary / Flickr.com

The time that the mother Shark is pregnant depends on the Shark species. Basking Sharks are pregnant for more than two years, while other Sharks, such as the Bonnet Head Shark, are pregnant for only a few months. The longest gestation period of any mammal is the Elephant, at 22 months.

When it comes time to give birth, the female Shark loses her appetite so she won't be tempted to eat her own pups.

A lengthy study completed in 2013 has found that Shark moms go home — to the place where they were born — to give birth to their young.

41. What animal lays the biggest eggs in the ocean?

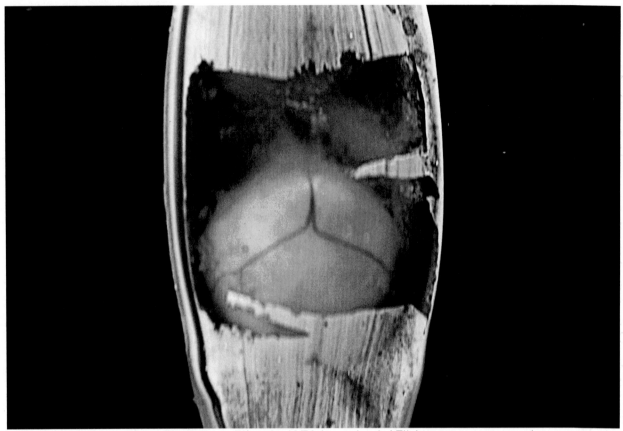
Shark Egg - Photo by IAEA Imagebank / Flickr.com

While the Ostrich lays the largest eggs on land, the Whale Shark lays the largest eggs in the world.

An egg from a Whale Shark measuring 14 inches in diameter was found in the Gulf of Mexico in 1953.

That is bigger more than 2 times the size of an ostrich egg and 1.5 times the size of a basketball!

42. Do Sharks swim while asleep?

Sleeping Nurse Shark - Photo by Skinned Mink / Flickr.com

Sleep walking causes problems for some people, but what about sleep swimming?

Some Sharks like the Nurse Shark and Bullhead Shark can stop swimming and be stationary. They pump water into their mouths using the muscles of their mouths, and push it out of their gills.

Most Sharks do need to swim constantly to keep water moving over their gills. They push water through their gills by swimming very fast with their mouths open.

These Sharks seem to have active periods and restful periods, rather than undergoing deep sleep like we do. They seem to be "sleep swimming," with parts of their brain less active or "resting" while the Shark remains swimming.

At least one study has shown that the Shark's spinal cord, controls swimming movements. This would make it possible for Sharks to swim while they are sleeping, and also rest their brains at the same time.

43. How often do Sharks eat?

Shark from underneath - Photo by Malkusch Markus / Flickr.com

Like Lions and other predators, Sharks usually kill only when they are hungry, which isn't very often.

Some Sharks can live a year without eating, living off the oil they stored in their bodies.

44. Which Sharks live the longest?

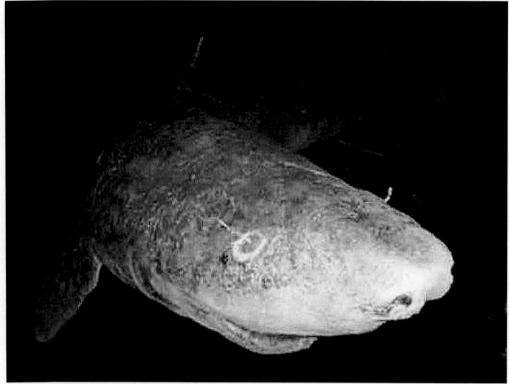

Greenland Shark - Photo by Justin / Flickr.com

Some estimates put the life span of Greenland Sharks at over 200 years!

Where does this number come from?

One study found Greenland Sharks grow less than 0,5 inch in a year.

A Greenland Shark that was captured and tagged off Greenland in 1936 was recaptured 16 years later. In that time, it had grown 2,26 inches longer. If these Sharks grow at about the same rate every year, that would make a mature 23-foot-long Shark over 200 years old!

This means the Greenland Shark may be one of the longest-lived animals on the planet.

Two other species of Shark live up to 100 years.

The Spiny or Piked Dogfish Shark. They usually live up to 70 years of age, but some may live until they are 100. Whale Sharks can also live up to 100 years.

45. What Shark is also called the Walking Shark?

The Epaulette Shark - Photo by Jim Capaldi, Wikimedia Commons

The Epaulette Shark is also known as the Walking Shark.

They use their fins to "walk" along the seabed. Epaulette Sharks live on or close to reefs. So this Shark moves along by what looks like walking.

It bends its body from side-to-side and pushes off of the seabed with its paddle-shaped pectoral and pelvic fins.

The Epaulette Shark is able to swim, but it often prefers to walk along the sandy or coral bottom even when the water is deep enough to allow it to swim freely.

This Shark is able to crawl out of the water to access isolated tidal pools.

Epaulette Sharks are largely nocturnal and are most active in low water.

46. What makes the Sevengill Shark different from all other Sharks?

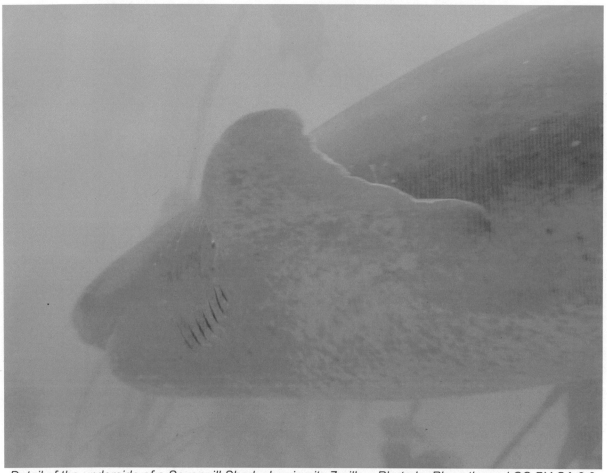

Detail of the underside of a Sevengill Shark showing its 7 gills – Photo by Pbsouthwood CC BY-SA 3.0, Wikimedia Commons

Almost all Sharks have 5 gill slits on each side of their bodies.

Only the Sevengill Shark has 7 gill slits on each side of its body – and that's where it gets its name.

47. Can you name the types of Shark in the Finding Nemo movie?

There were three Sharks in the Find Nemo film, who claimed that, "Fish are friends, not food." Can you name the 3 Sharks?

I.   Anchor was a Scalloped Hammerhead Shark.

Scalloped Hammerhead Shark - Photo by Barry Peters, CC BY 2.0, Wikimedia Commons

II.   Bruce was a Great White Shark.

Great White Shark - Photo by Sharkdiver.com, Public Domain, Wikimedia Commons

III.   Chum was a Shortfin Mako Shark.

Shortfin Mako Shark - Photo by jidanchaomian / Flickr.com

48. What Shark leaves a bite-mark shaped like a cookie cutter?

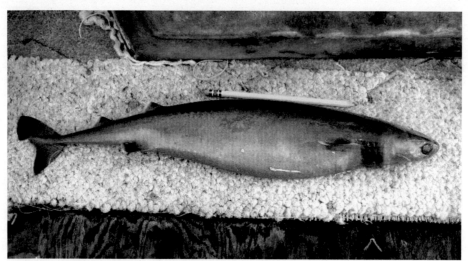

The Cookiecutter Shark - Photo by NOAA Observer Project, Public Domain, Wikimedia Commons

The Cookiecutter Shark gets its name from the cookie-cutter-like wounds it leaves in its prey.

It has a long, cylindrical body with a short, blunt nose and large eyes. Because of its shape it is also sometimes called the Cigar Shark.

To feed, the Shark attaches its mouth onto its victim and bites out a hunk of flesh using the row of serrated teeth on its lower jaw. It leaves a circular wound in its prey that looks like the hole a cookie cutter forms in dough. The wound it leaves is about 2 inches across and 2.5 inches deep.

This Shark is small: Males grow to a maximum of 16,5 inches, while females grow to 22 inches.

Marks made by Cookiecutter Sharks have been found on a wide variety of marine mammals and fishes, as well as on submarines and undersea cables.

Even other Sharks, including Great Whites, which are many times larger than the Cookiecutter Shark have been found with wounds left behind by Cookiecutter Sharks.

Pomfret Fish showing Cookiecutter Shark wounds - Photo by NOAA Observer Program, Public Domain, Wikimedia Commons

49. Why do some Sharks like to get a tan?

A Hammerhead Shark swimming just under the surface - Photo by Halibut Thyme, Public Domain, Wikimedia Commons

Hammerhead Sharks are one of the few animals on the planet that can tan.

One way that you tell old Hammerhead Sharks from young Hammerhead Sharks is from their tan.

Young Hammerhead Sharks get tans because they like to stay closer to the water's surface for long periods at a time.

Sometimes, they can even turn black.

They do not suffer from any sunburn either.

Their skin does not get damaged in any way from the sun. Scientists are studying young Hammerheads to find new ways of preventing skin disease in Humans.

50. Do you know these weird Shark facts?

Shark close up - Photo Public Domain / Pixabay.com

- Every individual Shark has its own personality and character. Some Sharks are shy and some are more social.
- Despite their fearsome reputation, Great Whites have only attacked 200 people across the world over the last 140 years, resulting in 77 deaths. Over 200 people are killed by Deer in the USA every year. So what is more dangerous – Great Whites or Deer?
- Sharks are older than trees. The earliest species that we could classify as a tree, lived around 350 million years ago, in forests where the Sahara Desert is now. But Sharks? They laugh at trees. They were around 50 million years before the first trees. Sharks have been on Earth for more than 400 million years.
- About 50 different Shark species glow in the dark. That's about 10% of all known Sharks.

51. If the Whale Shark is the largest fish. What is the 2nd largest?

Basking Shark just under the Ocean surface - Photo by Greg Skomal / NOAA Fisheries Service, Public Domain, Wikimedia Commons

The Basking Shark is the World's 2nd largest fish, after the Whale Shark, reaching longer than 35 feet in length. Like the Whale Shark, the Basking Shark is a filter feeder, eating only Plankton. It is found in all the world's warmer oceans.

It gets its name because it moves slowly feeding almost at the surface, almost basking in the layer of warmer water there. The Basking Shark is a slow moving Shark, moving at only 2 to 3 miles an hour.

This species of Shark has the smallest brain of any Shark relative to its body size. The Basking Shark's passive and inactive lifestyle can be linked to its lack of brain size.

If you liked this book...please tell others...

If you liked this book, please leave a review at your favorite bookseller's website. Please tell others what you liked about this book.

Visit www.TJRob.com for a FREE eBook and to see TJ Rob's other exciting books

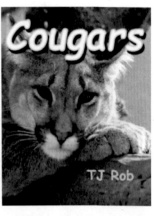

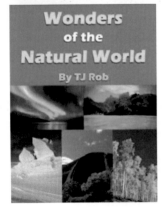
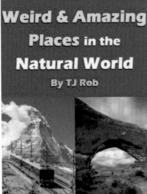

Made in the USA
Middletown, DE
28 March 2019